REFLECTIONS
from the C-Suite

REFLECTIONS
from the C-Suite

Opinions & Advice

Kevin M. Lewis

Copyright Notice

Contents

What Readers are Saying

"As president of a small business, I appreciate Kevin Lewis' "Reflections from the C-Suite." I found this book to be a quick and easy read—and extremely helpful to me as I "cross the chasm" to the next level of my business. Kevin's communication style is engaging and personable, and to the point. I appreciate the wisdom from the panel. They give great take-away/s from high level experience and lessons learned (sometimes the hard way). I feel that this book encourages me to take my business to the next level: it CAN be done!"

Sarah Meekhof, President, Capstone Consulting Group, LLC

"Reflections From the C-Suite: Opinions & Advice" by Kevin Lewis is a great read—worth keeping to review and read again and again. It is a book that makes you think. Each chapter has a focus, each comment is precise, concise, and to the point; there are deep and resonating messages that could be missed based on the brevity of the book. I highly recommend "Reflections From the C-Suite: Opinions & Advice" to all—students through retirees."

Dorian Anderson, President, DT Anderson Consulting LLC/Major General, US Army (ret.), Former Commander, Human Resources Command

"Eleanor Roosevelt said: "Learn from the mistakes of others. You can't live long enough to make them all yourself." In this short book, the author has captured lessons from top CEOs, as well as best practices. Key leadership principles are examined through multiple perspectives of successful leaders. A separate book could be written about each of the issues addressed. The writing style is accessible and compelling. A must-read for any leader. Bravo!!"

Colin Dunn, President, Colin K. Dunn & Associates/ Colonel, US Army (ret.), Former Commander, American Forces Network (Department of Defense's "Good Morning Vietnam" organization)

Introduction

THANK YOU! I do not take it for granted that you have parted with your hard earned money to purchase this book. My goal with this publication is to bring some straight-forward, direct advice and candid opinions from those who have served or are currently serving in the C-suite of corporate America. Hopefully you will come away with some helpful insights and nuggets that will assist you in your own leadership challenges, whether you are in the C-suite, headed in that direction, or leading a small, lean project team.

I have come to learn that if you maintain good, healthy relationships with people throughout your life, they will give you the shirts off their backs to help you. Such is the root and source of this publication. In my own struggles to get my business off the ground, I did not hesitate to seek advice from others with whom I have had the privilege to build and maintain a working and/or close relationship. These are friends and colleagues who have achieved much but speak very little about it. It became my desire to capture their thoughts and ideas and to share them.

In putting this publication together, I pondered several approaches, finally choosing one that I believe makes the flow of the book direct and the ideas easily comprehended: the panel approach. If you have attended any type of business conference, you have undoubtedly sat in on such an event. It is that of a moderator sitting on a stage with a panel of experts to whom the moderator poses questions, giving each person an opportunity to respond. Such is the approach taken here.

Following the next chapter wherein the backgrounds of the panel members contributing to this publication are presented, each subsequent chapter will present each member's response to the questions below:

What has been your deepest and/or most rewarding learning experience as a C-suite member?

How would you describe the differences, if any, between the picture you had of being a member of the C-suite vs. what you experienced after arriving there?

What has been your most agonizing experience and how did/have you progress through it?

Would you have prepared differently for the C-suite position? If so, how?

What new challenges do you see the C-suite facing in the near future?
What advice would you give to those about to step into the C-suite?

I do believe that somewhere within their responses you will find something that you will bring value to you and will be useful within your own enterprise, whether that enterprise be you as a solo-preneur or you as a senior leader within a large organization.

Now let me introduce the panel.

1

Panel Members

I want to go on the record here to thank each one of the panel members profusely for taking the time to provide their thoughts and ideas. As you might imagine, their bios are longer than what is presented here. I took the liberty of summarizing them.

After each bio, I have provided a "PERSONAL NOTE" to further share how I have been connected with each member.

Chris Cathcart is the President and CEO of the Consumer Specialty Products Association. Chris joined the Consumer Specialty Products Association (CSPA) as its president in January of 2000. During his tenure at the association, Chris initiated the formation of Product Care®, the industry's product stewardship program; and the founding of the Alliance for Consumer Education, the association's non-profit educational foundation for which he is a member of the Board of Trustees and serves as Secretary. Under his leadership, the Association has enjoyed a steady growth in membership and has achieved strong financial footing. Chris serves as President of the Association's insurance company, Consumer Specialties Insurance Company (CSI). He is also on the Board of Directors and Secretary of the Consumer Aerosol Products Council and is a board member of the Canadian Consumer Specialty Products Association.

Chris earned his Bachelor's of Science from the United States Military Academy at West Point, a Master's of Arts from Central Michigan University, and completed other postgraduate work at George Washington University.

Chris' C-suite experience includes 22 years within the chemical distribution industry and 12 years within the formulated consumer products industry.

> PERSONAL NOTE: Chris is a classmate. He was very gracious to invite my daughter, currently a college student, to interview with his organization for a summer internship, where she is now working at the time of this publication. She supports the Alliance for Consumer Education, overseeing its social media campaign.

Bill Higgs is one of three founders of Mustang Engineering, a 5000-person engineering design company serving the energy industry. In 1992, Mustang was ranked as the 42nd company in Inc. Magazine's "500 Fastest Growing Companies in America" and was ranked as the number one Engineering firm. Mustang is currently Houston's largest pure engineering company and a world leader serving the oil and gas industry worldwide.

Bill, along with Mustang partner Paul Redmon, received the Engineering and Construction Contracting Association's (ECC) 2004 Achievement Award in recognition of "Visionary Leadership in the Process Industry". Bill is an accomplished speaker, having spoken at multiple venues to include Texas A&M's 61st annual Instrumentation Symposium, the Offshore Europe 2005 conference, the Offshore Technology Conference (OTC), the ECC annual conference, and the 2004 annual Rice Global Forum for Engineering and Construction.

Bill began his career in the oil and gas industry in 1979 as an engineer, concentrating on offshore Gulf of Mexico projects and working for two local engineering firms before helping launch Mustang in 1987. He received a Texas Professional Mechanical Engineers license in 1987 by testing.

Bill is a 1974 Distinguished Graduate of the United States Military Academy at West Point, graduating at the top 5% of his class at West Point. He was runner-up in the Rhodes scholarship competition. Higgs has served

West Point as a member of its Board of Directors Fund Committee.

Bill's C-suite experience includes 21 years in the oil and gas Industry from 1987 through 2008.

> PERSONAL NOTE: I have not had the privilege of working directly with Bill. However, given that we are also classmates and, upon the recommendation of a close mutual friend, I reached out to him to seek his input for this project. He was more than willing to contribute.

Joshua S. Levine is a Managing Director of Kita Capital Management, LLC, an information technology investing, operating, consulting and research firm, since 2006. He is CTO and a Director of Americans Elect, a non-partisan effort to use the Internet to nominate a presidential ticket for every state ballot in 2012. The website AmericansElect.org won the 2012 SxSW (South by Southwest) People's Choice award, awarded to Groupon in 2011. From 2007, until its exit with Investment Technology Group (ITG) in 2010, he was the CEO and a Director of ESP Technologies Corp., a financial technology provider to asset managers. He joined ESP as CEO and invested with Credit Suisse, Bear Stearns and Susquehanna Growth Equity. Under his leadership, annual revenues grew from $12 million in 2006 to over $60 million in 2010, and made the Inc. 5000, the Red Herring North America 100, and Deloitte's Technology

Fast 500 lists. Levine was also a finalist for the 2009 Ernst & Young Entrepreneur of the Year.

His awards include: InfoWorld's "Top 25 most influential CTO's", CIO magazine's "CIO 100", CIO Forum's "Top 20 financial IT executives", Keynote's best transaction speed and reliability, a "Webby" for the best banking and bill pay on the internet, and an American Business Award "Stevie" for the best technology team.

He co-authored a textbook, "Application Systems in APL", published by Prentice-Hall. Levine is a graduate of the Bronx High School of Science and dropped out of Syracuse University to pursue a career in computing. In 2001, he received an honorary D.Sc. from the University of Georgia, Southern Polytechnic State University. Levine currently holds FINRA license Series 7, 63 and 24.

Josh's C-suite experience includes serving as a CTO and CEO within the financial services industry since 1997.

> PERSONAL NOTE: I had privilege of working as the program officer in support of a defense-related study for the National Research Council in Washington, DC. Josh was a member of the study panel.

Patrick A. McBrayer is President and Chief Executive Officer of AxioMed™ Spine Corporation of Garfield Heights, Ohio. AxioMed is a medical device company focused on restoring the native function of the spine.

He is also a Founder of Transave Inc., a biotechnology company focused on the site specific treatment of lung disease. Prior to joining Xylos, Mr. McBrayer served as President and CEO of Exogen, Inc., a company focused on the non-invasive treatment of musculoskeletal injury and disease, which was acquired by Smith & Nephew, Inc. in 1999. He received the Thomas Alva Edison Patent Award in 1998 for a biological implant for bone repair that is now a market leading product. Prior to joining Osteotech, Mr. McBrayer held positions of increasing responsibility for Johnson & Johnson, Inc.

He has over 20 years healthcare senior management experience and served as an Infantry Officer Company Commander in the U.S. Army prior to beginning his business career. A 1974 graduate of the United States Military Academy, Mr. McBrayer also served on West Point's Association of Graduates Board of Trustees.

Pat's C-suite experience includes serving as a Chief Executive for emerging, venture backed medical companies for 25 years.

> PERSONAL NOTE: Pat is also a classmate.
> We have worked together on a gift selection
> and fundraising project for our West Point
> class.

James (Jay) McConville is the Executive Vice President for Strategy and Business Development at Chandler/May, Inc. and the Chairman of the Board of AME Unmanned Air Systems, Inc. a Chandler/May company. The combined companies specialize in the design, development and manufacture of unmanned aircraft systems (UAS), UAS Ground Control Systems, and Intelligence, Surveillance and Reconnaissance (ISR) mission management solutions for defense and intelligence customers. Jay is the former President and CEO of AME Unmanned Systems (then called "AeroMech Engineering"), and served four years as the Vice President for Strategy and Business Development for Chandler/May. Before joining Chandler/May, Jay was the Vice President of Reconnaissance and Surveillance within a major defense firm, directing over $300M per year of the company's systems integration and engineering business. He has served in various other industry positions supporting defense agencies and the national intelligence community for over 15 years.

Jay is the President of the Washington DC Chapter of the Association of Unmanned Vehicle Systems International (AUVSI) and also serves on the Mt. Vernon-Lee Chamber of Commerce Board of Directors. Jay has a Bachelors of Science from George Mason University and a Master of Science in Strategic Intelligence from the Defense Intelligence College, Washington, DC.

Jay's C-suite experience includes 13 months as CEO.

PERSONAL NOTE: I currently serve with Jay on the board of directors of the Mt. Vernon-Lee Chamber of Commerce in

Alexandria, VA. I initially met Jay when he ran for a local elective office.

Ronald J. Steptoe is the Chairman and CEO of the Steptoe Group LLC, a Service Disabled Veteran-owned company. He started the Steptoe Group to bring healthcare advocacy curriculum and training to the federal sector marketplace. He is a Service Disabled Veteran and is leveraging his extensive private sector business experience in providing management and technical solutions to the Government and Private sectors.

As CEO, Ronald has established innovative partnerships with National Medical Association, Department of Continuing Education, Accreditation Council of Continuing Medical Education, and the International Association of Continuing Education and Training to provide a "medically-accredited military culture, cultural competency, and patient-provider communication in the clinical setting" educational training program for health and service support providers with the expertise and capacity to deliver high-quality services that are patient-centered, evidence based and address the health needs of vulnerable population within the military and veteran communities. Ron serves on the Board of Directors of USA Cares, Inc (a Veterans Service Organization).

He is a 1987 graduate from the United States Military Academy, West Point, NY, subsequently serving as a commissioned officer.

Ron's C-suite experience includes serving as a COO and CEO since 2008.

> PERSONAL NOTE: My company has partnered with Ron's firm in the pursuit of consulting opportunities focused on organizational performance improvement. His work in support of Wounded Warriors dovetails very closely with my volunteer efforts in support of that community.

Lee A. Van Arsdale has served as a Soldier and business executive. As a Soldier his assignments were primarily in Special Forces, with 11 years spent in the First Special Forces Operational Detachment-Delta (Airborne). In the course of his 25 year Army career, Lee served in three combat zones in leadership positions, and was decorated for valor with the Silver Star and with the Purple Heart for wounds received in combat. Additionally, he participated in numerous classified operations, on a global scale, while in a leadership capacity.

Following his military career, Lee was the Assistant General Manager for National Security Response at the Bechtel Nevada Corporation; he incorporated Unconventional Solutions, Inc., a private consulting firm; he was the founding Executive Director of the University of Nevada Las Vegas Institute for Security Studies, and was the Chief Executive Officer of Triple Canopy, Inc., an integrated security solutions company.

Lee also served as the military consultant to the Ridley Scott film "Black Hawk Down" and appeared in the documentary "The True Story of Blackhawk Down". He now serves on the boards of select companies.

Lee's C-suite experience includes 9 years in various c-suite positions within consulting, government contracting, and academia.

> PERSONAL NOTE: Lee, also a classmate, was one of the first people I met during the early stages of my business. He opened doors for me and was very gracious with his time. I also enjoyed picking his brain about his experiences in Mogadishu during the events that were depicted in the movie "Black Hawk Down". He is as an American hero. (*Lee, I know you don't like my saying that. But this is my book . . . and I get the last word here.*)

Don Zacherl founded T3 Technologies in March 2004 based on a number of governing principles that continue to drive its development: Trusted, Talented, and Tireless. Don has extensive leadership and management experience in Military, Non-profit, and Corporate organizations. Don was chosen by "ComputerWorld" magazine as one of the 100 Premier Technology Leaders in the United States.

His company was recognized twice by Dun and Bradstreet 'Open Ratings' for Outstanding Customer

Service, 2004 and 2007 and chosen as "Outstanding American by Choice" by the Department of Homeland Security, 2008.

He is a graduate of the United States Military Academy at West Point, earning a Bachelors of Science degree in engineering. He holds an MA in Mathematics and Computer Science from Hofstra University and an MBA from George Washington University. He was selected for Beta Gamma Sigma Honor Society. His other accomplishments include graduating from the CIO Executive Program at Stanford University and completing the Business Model Development program at Aresty Institute of the Wharton School of Business. He is a Microsoft Certified Systems Engineer.; a PMI Certified Project Management Professional (PMP); and a Lean Six Sigma Master Black Belt from Villanova University.

Don's C-suite experience includes: two years as CTO for a Non-Profit Lobbying Organization; three years as COO of a Commercial Software company; and five years as the CEO of a Management Consulting.

> PERSONAL NOTE: Don, also a classmate (who always finds himself at the bottom of any and every list because of his name) provided me with the initial encouragement to step out and establish my enterprise. His firm and mine have also partnered together in the pursuit of consulting opportunities.

2

Most Rewarding Experience

What has been your deepest and/or most rewarding learning experience as a C-suite member?

CHRIS: Figuring out that the key to success is surrounding myself with excellent people and helping them advance.

BILL: My most rewarding learning experience was to find out that staying true to our beliefs and philosophies could change people. Spouses would come up to me at parties and say that their husband had become a better person since working at Mustang. These conversations would send a tingle up my spine as that seemed like the highest level of achievement for a company.

JOSH: The best part of senior management is having the opportunity to lead with impact. After 9/11, when everything was topsy-turvy, leading colleagues to focus on a positive future, handling the business uncertainty and achieving that future, were the most rewarding and impactful experiences I've ever had.

PAT: When you are in the patient care business it is most rewarding when an innovative technology makes an impact on patients and their medical care professionals. In each of my companies, my colleagues and I have witnessed surgeries, treatments and intervention that have made a positive impact on the medical outcomes of patients. It is also rewarding to know that the team you helped assemble was responsible for the invention, testing, development and introduction of products that are unique in their respective fields.

JAY: The most rewarding experience was in the transformation of the company from a small, opportunity-based based business to a corporation with a larger vision that was able to pursue strategic business based on a long-term plan. The movement of any company from one that lives day-to-day to one that sets its market direction is very difficult, and has been described as "crossing the chasm." Making this transition requires changes in culture, back office systems, engineering and production processes, and business development—not to mention overall strategy. When such a transition occurs, the business stops living for the next small sale, and begins to set its own market direction, winning larger and more enduring work and providing better services to their customers.

RON: I think my biggest learning experience has been to learn to trust your vision and then to trust the mission you put behind the vision. Then trusting good people to carry out the mission which should carry out your vision. I've learned that it's okay that some people come and some people go. At the end of the day you keep that ship moving and you're going to find that people will self-select themselves to stay with you and make sure the mission is carried through. And that takes time. You have to be able to handle that process. People who embrace your vision provide value to your team. And you never devalue that. Always appreciate people for the time they were with you. Just be emotionally ready for that process. I think the biggest and the deepest learning experience is to trust the mission you put together. Then trust the people that you put behind making that mission happen because you can't do it by yourself.

LEE: My most rewarding learning experience as a CEO occurred when I took over a company with no infrastructure and little sense of teamwork, so I learned the hard way the importance of implementing an infrastructure while running the business.

DON: aking lasting change, either leading a turn around, managing operations in a rapidly growing start up, or making sustained impact on a client.

3

C-Suite Reality

How would you describe the differences, if any, between the picture you had of being a member of the C-suite vs. what you experienced after arriving there?

CHRIS: It is different when you are in the driver's seat. It is one thing to see how someone else develops a vision for an organization, gets buy in and ownership from his team and then work with them as they attain that vision through a well-executed plan. When it is your turn, it is show time.

BILL: The picture I had was of a detached leadership team that had trouble communicating with the people. I was afraid of becoming part of that picture due to the responsibilities and pressures of the C-suite. I found that with diligence I could paint the picture I envisioned of an uplifting, engaged management team.

JOSH: I always thought that senior management was the reward in your career. While it is a great opportunity, it comes with the heavy burden of leadership and all it entails.

PAT: If you enter as CEO of a company with established founders and the beginning of a culture, you must be careful to shepherd change in lieu of radical alteration (unless you have a turn—around candidate). Those with the early experience of founding the company are valuable and I have always approached these situations as a partner. You are still in charge but the management style should be a guiding force not a sledge hammer.

JAY: I had a lot of experience as a VP, so I was not totally unprepared for the scope of the work of the CEO. That said, having a say about every decision in the company was a big adjustment. The other major adjustment was the need to deal with the Board of Directors and the continuous pressure of the quarterly financial report. As a VP I tended to look at the fiscal year in achieving my goals. As CEO and now as Chairman my focus is on meeting every financial metric in every month and every quarter. A very positive difference was in my ability to strategically set the direction for the company through investment in research and development and new business pursuits. We made major facility and production investments based on this new strategy and that has been an exciting endeavor. Setting a strategy that stands the test of time is key to this. If you are continually changing your strategy, you may not really have one!

RON: It's harder than I thought because you not only have to deal with the product development, you have to deal with how you would finance your product's production. Where is the capital going to come from? How do you raise the capital? How do you make sure that you have an effective marketing effort behind what you're doing? And how do you make sure the production is taken care of? How do you deal with distribution? How do you deal with the HR components of making all of that happen? As an entrepreneur, particularly if you're trying to build a system that is going to be national and have the impact that you want it to have, you have to deal with all of those particular dynamics. In recent years, I've had to address these issues. I'm not an expert, but my acumen in these areas has improved and deepened. I have enough of an understanding that, when I get those experts on board, I am now more effective and overseeing their efforts in their respective domains.

LEE: The company I took over had phenomenal success in its first year, and then crashed during the second. I took over after the crash, and was surprised to find out that there was no infrastructure in place, i.e., no policies or procedures, a dysfunctional IT platform, incomplete financial records and procedures, a non-functioning HR department, etc.

DON: I don't think I had a lot of illusions, since I had done about everything. I think that getting to the 'C-suite' is not a destination; it is only a milestone on a journey, to use the cliché. I don't think I had a vision of 'arriving'; it is more like, 'where do I want to go next?'

4

Most Agonizing Experience

What has been your most agonizing experience and how did/have you progress through it?

CHRIS: It is hard to remove a person from a position they want (a position to which they have trained and aspired, but they simply are not equipped to handle.) This can be a win/win if I am able to redirect the person to move along a path that calls on their greatest talents.

BILL: As we had built a strong culture and moved an industry to a new place, we later felt that we needed to sell the company. We wanted to sell into an upturn in the industry and not lose people, clients or projects during the process. Our Merger & Acquisitions (M&A)

team from Chase told us that we would have to keep everything secret as we worked through the sale process for eight months. We had built up a lot of trust with our people, clients and vendors and did not feel that we could lie to them as information would invariably get out, even if not confirmed. We told the M&A team that we wanted to announce our intentions and to call what we were doing our "Adopt-a-Parent" program. The M&A team strongly recommended against this as it would significantly erode the value of the company, as when people would start to leave and clients would withhold projects while they waited to see what would happen. I was given the job of "selling" our Adopt a Parent program to our people, our clients and the industry. I prepared a pamphlet (my Master's Thesis) explaining what we were about to do. The real agonizing part was not knowing how the message would be received.

At our normal Monday morning operations meeting I brought my Minister to open with prayer for what we were about to undertake. Then I handed out the pamphlets, let the managers thumb through them and then I walked them through the specifics. I opened the floor to questions which my senior management colleagues and I answered. We told them that no one in the industry knew what we were about to undertake. We wanted the managers to take enough pamphlets for their people and go conduct meetings to explain our plan. We had over three hundred people out of a thousand at our firm that had arrived due to sales of engineering companies that had gone very poorly. They still had significant wounds from those experiences and this was going to be bad news to them. I attended the meeting with one large group of such people and was asked what they could say about this outside of the company. I told them that if they agreed with everything in the pamphlet and were supportive, to feel free to call anyone they chose when they left the meeting. If they thought everything presented was hogwash and this process was going to be horrible in their eyes, then I asked that they discuss the pamphlet with their spouse and sleep on it. In the morning if they still had significant misgivings, I suggested that they please talk over those issues with someone they trusted at the company. If they still thought it was a horrible idea, then they were free to call anyone they wanted to express their feelings.

I told them that I was going to send an email to all of our clients that afternoon and start calling on them to give them a copy of the pamphlet and review it with them. The next day I went into a monthly project review meeting being held at our company's site on a project called Mica. The project was co-owned by BP and Exxon with BP being in charge of development. BP had bought Amoco and Exxon was in the process of buying Mobil. Representatives from all four oil companies were in the room when I handed out the pamphlets and walked them through what we were doing. At the end, one of the Mobil engineers asked if I would create a pamphlet like this for the ExxonMobil merger which got great laughs from everyone as the BP-Amoco merger had been very lacking on communication with the people. By Thursday the company's sale was a non-event within company itself and within the industry. All parties commented that we had a good plan that would be good for both our people and client projects going forward. Everyone went back to work trusting that our company would figure out how to implement their Adopt-a-Parent program successfully.

JOSH: Having to stand in front of my department and tell them there would be no bonuses because our CEO got embroiled in a controversy during a year where we had losses and the stock price had fallen to $2.62 from $60. How did I get through it? By being honest, acknowledging how awful it was and encouraging them that we'll get through it together.

PAT: Raising venture capital is never easy, regardless of the promise of your company. You have to prepare your staff and employees for the rigorous and sometimes frightening experience. Patience is a virtue in this regard but it is sometimes difficult to keep everyone focused when you have a few months of cash on hand and the next round of financing still in progress. Also in every medical company you face some challenges with new products. You have to be a calming force but be prepared to address issues quickly and decisively. In our business, bad news doesn't get better with age so I want to know it STAT (immediately).

JAY: Realigning the company to a more strategic vision required changes in personnel—including some very senior people. People who were both comfortable and valuable in the short-term business were not necessarily the right people to move the company to a new level. Separating these people from the company was the most difficult thing I had to do.

Second to that was the requirement to "no-bid" on business that traditionally paid some of the bills, but was short term, low profit, and in fact a distraction from our strategic direction. Company leaders were hesitant to give up on customers who had traditionally supported our company with small dollar sales, but in order to leverage our investment capital against larger more strategic customers, we had to make those tough decisions. The company had become somewhat addicted to that revenue, so foregoing it—even for much larger opportunities—was a difficult cultural change.

RON: Given the healthcare focus of our firm with services being delivered to ultimately serve the veteran and Wounded Warrior community, I think the most agonizing experience that I've had relates to soldiers' experiencing post traumatic stress disorder, traumatic brain injury and helping them get their lives back on track. The key question for us is this: What are some of the products and services that could be brought to the market to help them or help the people that are there to serve them? Our business model is very much a policy driven type of business where we try to bring those solutions to the table. What has been extremely frustrating is when policy hasn't matched up effectively with what the market is demanding. Yet you push ahead, knowing that at some point, the policy and market alignment will eventually come.

LEE: Having to fire some of the key leaders, who were friends of mine. You progress through it by keeping in mind the fact that when you sign on as the CEO, the interests of the company come first.

DON: Losing employees, for any reason, is the hardest thing. I don't think it gets easier, either, with time. It is a great motivator, though, to hire the right folks and to keep the business going. Sometimes people quit, sometimes they had to get fired, but the hardest is when they haven't done anything wrong, but can't adapt to new requirements.

5

Retroactive Preparation

Would you have prepared differently for the C-suite position? If so, how?

CHRIS: I was fortunate to have served in the military. The leadership opportunities and experience received there helped prepare me for the career path I chose.

BILL: I had wanted to get an MBA and had signed up to do it while working though a program offered by HBU in Houston. Two weeks before the course started I was diagnosed with an awfully aggressive cancer (11% survival rate) and spent a year at MD Anderson Cancer Center doing radiation and experimental chemotherapy. Thankfully MD Anderson and

Dr. Melvin Samuels helped me "Make Cancer History". Other than an MBA, I think I was fully prepared from my Boy Scout, Church, West Point, Ranger, Army, and oilfield experience.

JOSH: The many keys to successful management include networking, focusing on the task, an understanding of the role, and communicating. Don't wait until you get there before learning these. It will be too late.

PAT: I went straight from the Army into business. Perhaps business school would have helped prepare me better on the financial aspects of being a CEO. I learned the hard way.

JAY: The biggest hurdle for me was the financial systems hurdle. Understanding the world of the CFO is very difficult for one who has come up via the operations or business development side of an organization. The terminology was new, the analysis sometimes foreign, and the emphasis on profit versus revenue was a very important lesson to learn.

RON: I didn't arrive at the C-Suite by choice. However, I think I always wanted to be in a C-Suite. It was one of the reasons why I wanted to attend the Academy. I wanted to be in the military to learn how to develop those leadership skills, knowing that one day whether it was after five years or after retirement. At some point I was going to be in the marketplace. What I found is that people that were successful in the marketplace had military experience. So now that I think about it, I actually did prepare myself. So would I have done anything differently? I don't think that I would have. I think that every experience I've had has enabled me to bring a uniqueness into the marketplace.

LEE: Yes, I would have done a far more thorough check on the state of the company before taking over.

DON: I don't think so. I didn't have a plan to prepare for C level positions. I just wanted to do more and do it better. I was a little surprised, actually, when I was first recruited and had to talk to headhunters.

6

New Challenges

What new challenges do you see the C-suite facing in the near future?

CHRIS: In public businesses and organizations, CEOs will be challenged by Boards in areas that have been traditionally in the strict domain of the CEO. The rules of the game are changing and those CEOs who want to survive and help their organizations thrive will need to understand these changes.

BILL: The key challenge will be to differentiate from worldwide competitors by providing better value and an "experience" that can be felt as being different. The entire organization has to be aligned to make this happen and that takes strong leadership.

JOSH: In today's instant-on world, it's harder and harder to take the long term view—at least without short term deliverables. A long term strategy must be coupled with short term projects with results in order to succeed.

PAT: In the venture start up business, access to capital will get more difficult than it is now. I predict many promising new companies will not make it unless the IPO market improves and gives venture capital some needed wins. Now only the best of the best get funded, particularly if you have a technology with a long regulatory pathway.

JAY: The major challenge is not new. Each company needs to find its strategic position, define its market, and figure out how to differentiate itself in that market. There are many revenue opportunities, but the C-Suite leader needs to do more than be opportunity driven. You need to set the direction—long term—for your organization and develop a strategy that stands the test of time within a competitive market. This requires analysis, a deep understanding of the market, and a little luck. Decisions based on those factors are often hard to make, as they are very uncertain and often go against the advice of some of your more seasoned employees. Each C-suite leader needs to be clear on "what this company does" and that is sometimes difficult. If you are not clear, then the company is opportunity, vice strategy, driven. Opportunity driven companies cannot scale up, and growth will be limited if you pursue this path.

RON: Things are going to change very fast. I'm not sure what the life cycle is going to be for products and services particularly when you look at medicine and healthcare services. The market is going to look a lot different. I think the global market is going to be a lot closer. And I think that we're going to have to be open to diversity of thought and ideas. I think that we need to have a keen interest in making sure that we look after America and what we do. We're in a global economy. The U.S. only represents a small percentage of the marketplace. So the question is, how is that C-Suite person going to get the experience they need to understand the global market? This is vital in order to compete effectively.

LEE: Continued rapid changes in telecommunications will require the C-suite to stay in front of the curve. The ability for anyone in the company, as well as clients and competition, to communicate anywhere/anytime presents challenges in terms of cyber security, maintaining confidentiality, staying on message, etc. Having said that, there are also numerous opportunities presented; the C-suite has to be smart enough to take advantage of them.

DON: Selecting my replacement!

7

Advice for Future
C-Suite Occupants

What advice would you give to those about to step into the C-suite?

CHRIS: Don't take yourself too seriously. Learn everything you can about the business and its future potential. Attract, reward and retain the best people.

BILL: Before you step in, sit down and write what you like and dislike about the C-suite members you have known in the past. Write down what you value and what you want the organization to value. Then once there, look at these lists once a quarter to ensure you are not "incrementing" into the negative things on your lists.

JOSH: Start NOW in identifying and developing the skills that you will need. Read "Leading at the Edge", a comparison of two journeys including Shackleton's successful Antarctic expedition.

PAT: Read good books on business, political and military leaders. I recommended to my staff that they read the biography "Brute" on Marine General Krulak, one of the most creative and innovative leaders this nation has had. He was also a visionary and should have been listened to more closely during Vietnam. One can draw many parallels in your business from great leaders from all professions. You can always learn from others' mistakes as well. Read the critically reviewed books on business failures.

JAY: You are not an accountant, you are not a program manager, and you are not a business developer. You are the leader of the organization who is expected to see the bigger picture, set the direction, and develop the plans, investment strategies, and the team needed to accomplish the big goals. Don't get mired in the details. Take some time each day to look at the bigger picture. What is it you want to accomplish? How will you make your organization a leader in your market? What financial metrics do you need to achieve? What business do you need to win to make those objectives—both short and long term? What business improvements do you need to make to win that business?

What investments are needed to execute that business after you win? This is your job—don't try to do everyone else's job. Hire the others needed to execute and remember to think big.

RON: Be flexible and be willing to take the time to learn the skill sets of where you're at. I tell folks that the important thing is to be a preneur. There's an entrepreneur or intrapreneur. You want to be a creator and there's value in organizations where you're the preneur and you make things happen. As you do that, you learn the process of understanding what takes to bring value to an organization. By the same token, those same skill sets apply when you're out in the marketplace. Everything that you do brings value to your experience. Once you have that experience, you have to trust your vision. If you feel very comfortable with what you're doing, you feel that you've been prepared. One thing will lead to the next that will lead you to the next that will lead you to the next. You just have to have that very clear vision of what you're trying to do, where you're trying to go to. Trust yourself and your skill set. Embrace every opportunity to learn and do it 100% no matter what it is because there's value in that learning.

LEE: Don't take yourself too seriously; stay grounded; communicate with subordinates at every opportunity. I always remember the advice of Richard Branson of Virgin Atlantic et al. The day I, as the CEO, learn to build a great spreadsheet is the day my company is doomed!

DON: Keep doing what you do best, hire great people to do what you can't do well, and help any learner who wants to be a leader.

8

Final Comments

What final thoughts do you have? Any recommended reading? Any message to those young folks entering the business area?

CHRIS: For reading material, I recommend "Team of Rivals", by Doris Kearns Goodwin, which covers Lincoln and his cabinet; and "Unbroken", by Laura Hillenbrand about WW2 POW Louis Zamparini, and how he persevered against unimaginable torture and his personal success post WW2. My guidance to new business grads: set your moral compass and stick to it. Ethics in business leadership is paramount—don't let anyone persuade you otherwise. Also, when things go south, don't blame others—leaders must take responsibility. I think of Eisenhower's back up statement in case D-Day failed.

BILL: When you build people up and they feel the trust, they will do the little things that make an organization great . . . when no one is looking.

JOSH: Leadership is rewarding and all it takes is some wisdom and the conviction to lead. For reading, I recommend "Leading at the Edge" by Dennis Perkins.

PAT: First, let me offer this thought from the Chinese philosopher Lao Tsu, Sixth Century B.C: "A Good Leader's Aim Is To Open People's Hearts, Fill Their Stomachs, Calm Their Wills And Brace Their Bones." In terms of reading, I have also encouraged my staff over the years to read Manchester's "American Caesar" and recently "Brute: The Life of Victor Krulak" by Robert Coram. General Krulak was a great visionary as well as a leader (Higgin's boats WWII and helicopter Korean war). As with MacArthur, you can see how a leader with a vision can create change and influence history. I think Sun Tzu's "The Art of War" is instructive in business. Ralph Sawyer's translation is a good one.

The ethics message is so important to MBAs and young executives starting out in business. I give all my employees General Colin Powell's "Rules" and refer to it often in real world situations so they see the relevance. Michael Lewis's "The Big Short" and his earlier "Liar's Poker" are good books that reinforce the role of ethics in business and danger of the lack thereof.

JAY: I recall a business school case that I studied. Ivory Snow was dominating the market in laundry soap. Tide wanted to break into that market but was having limited success. So Tide developed the word "detergent" (which basically means "artificial soap") and defined a new market. Now Tide is the leader in laundry detergent—and laundry soap is a distant also-ran. In that example we find the true role of the CEO. Set your company's direction, define your market, and win it. All the rest is just details.

For reading, in addition to faithful reading of the relevant industry publications (in my case ISR Magazine, Unmanned Systems Magazine, and C4ISR Journal) I have always favored biographies of great leaders. From their example of leadership in crisis many lessons can be taken. "Warlord" by Carlo D'Este on Winston Churchill is a particular favorite, as is "With Malice Towards None", Stephen Oates' biography of Abraham Lincoln. Of course David McCullough's books are on the top of the list—"John Adams," "1776" and even "Truman" which is long but worth the wait. I've never been a big reader of business books, but "Leading Out Loud" by Pearce is a good one, as is "The Seven Habits of Highly Effective People" by Stephen Covey (which I quote from all the time).

For new business graduates, my advice is this: You earn your success through hard work, expertise, and thoughtful, yet bold, decision making—not by manipulation or scheming. If you keep your eye on the success of your business, your own success will follow. Don't expect to be CEO in 2 years. Learn the business, learn what makes it successful and what keeps it from success. Success means delivering a quality product or service profitably (don't forget the profit part!). Focus on that and work hard and smart to achieve it. Become irreplaceable to management. If you do that, success will come to you (although there will be setbacks, there always are).

RON: Let me highlight the importance and value of "intellectual property" as highlighted in the Rich Dad's Advisors series: "Protecting Your #1 Asset—Creating Fortunes from Your Ideas, An Intellectual Property Handbook"—by Michael A. Lechter, ESQ. The second book I recommend is: "Strategic Partnerships, An Entrepreneur's Guide to Joint Ventures and Alliances—by Robert L. Wallace. Lastly,

I would state to new graduates that it is critical that you embrace the mindset of a "preneur" (a creator) who brings value to an organization via actionable ideas. Thus, you can be an intrapreneur or an entrepreneur. An Intrapreneur is a person within a corporation who takes direct responsibility for turning an idea into a profitable, finished product through assertive risk-taking and innovation. An Entrepreneur is a person who is willing to help launch a new venture or enterprise and accepts full responsibility for the outcome. Each brings great value to organizations and society.

LEE: To those young people entering the business world, it is critically important that you have a legal, moral, and ethical foundation. If everything you were taught in business school isn't applied on this foundation, then it is all for naught. My experience with business school grads and MBAs is that they don't know much about leadership. In many cases they know the theories of program management, but not much about people. For reading, I recommend the Wall Street Journal, and biographies of people like George Washington, George Marshall, George Patton, Robert Frederick, Grant & Lee, Black Jack Pershing, Douglas MacArthur . . . in short, leaders who went through the crucible.

DON: Life is a roller coaster and you have no choice about whether you are going for the ride. You may as well hang on and enjoy it!

9

Author Reflections

I find it very difficult to call myself "author" given that all I have done is capture the intellectual property of those with whom I have been blessed to be associated and used a popular medium to disseminate it. Nonetheless, I do have some closing points I'd like to share.

Remember that there is always something to be gained in every relationship, even if it is a relationship you would like to forget. Learning can be at its best when the struggle is at its worst . . . IF you are prepared to learn.

We live in a busy . . . no . . . a chaotic world. Even so, work hard to maintain those relationships that are valuable to you. Find a way to bring value to them when possible.

Hopefully this book has brought some value to you. Our plan at LMK Partners LLC is to publish a series of books on topics that can assist emerging leaders in their own personal and organizational development. We will also be utilizing the associated research as a part of our case study work in support of clients who are seeking to improve and enhance their organizations and teams via our productivity enhancement workshops. This publication will be made available as a print-on-demand hardcopy book, enabling us to leave behind an in-depth "calling card".

Allow me to make an offer to you. You and your organization have developed highly valuable intellectual property. It is in your collective heads, emails, white papers, and other forms of communication that you utilize. Allow us to work with you in capturing that IP and turning it into a publication that you can use as your own calling card. It will make a deep first impression with prospective clients and distinguish you from your competitors. Remember that saying, "You don't get a second chance to make a first impression"? This will make your first impression a lasting one.

I leave you with these words of wisdom from the Book of Proverbs:

He who walks with the wise grows wise.

I hope this short walk with my colleagues has made you wiser.

About the Author

Kevin Lewis is the CEO and Managing Partner of LMK Partners LLC, a veteran-owned enterprise. His firm delivers services in the area of organizational improvement, productivity analysis, and change management. His career includes service as a combat arms officer in the U.S. Army and 30+ years in the competitive world of information technology, collaborative study research, and management consulting.

His experience encompasses his serving on U.S. delegations to international organizations, developing techno-policy in collaboration with international governance bodies such as the ISO and the European Commission, and facilitating study programs for the National Research Council. During his time at the NRC, he recruited and collaborated with C-level industry leaders, retired military flag officers, and former federal political appointees.

He also served as the CEO/Managing Director for IMS International, Inc., a not-for-profit organization charged with coordinating and facilitating the development and sharing of intellectual property across international boundaries. His most recent engagement has been to support the military in the re-design and pilot testing of the Transition Assistance Program, a program that supports veterans as they transition into civilian careers.

In addition to managing the delivery of his firm's services, he has taken on the personal mission of working as a coaching partner with today's emerging senior business leaders. "The pace of today's business climate is causing many leaders to stumble, costing them time, money, and more importantly valued relationships. I want to bring my own lessons learned to the table to assist these leaders in becoming more effective and productive . . . and help them get a good night's rest."

Kevin is a Certified Human Behavior Consultant, a Board Certified Coach (Center for Credentialing and Education), and DISC trainer/facilitator. He received his coaching certification and DISC training through the Christian Coach Institute LLC where, as a CCI alumni member, he receives critical ongoing support and education to maintain his effectiveness as a coach and trainer.

He received his undergraduate degree from the United States Military Academy at West Point and his graduate degree in business administration from Central Michigan University in Mt. Pleasant, Michigan.

He is an author and speaker. He serves as an adjunct professor for the School of Business at Northern Virginia Community College and is on the Board of Directors for the Mount Vernon-Lee Chamber of Commerce. He also volunteers as a Wounded Warrior mentor.

Appendix

Below are the full biographies of each of the contributors:

Chris Cathcart,
President/CEO, Consumer Specialty Products Association

Chris Cathcart joined the Consumer Specialty Products Association (CSPA) as its president in January of 2000. During his tenure at the association, Cathcart initiated the formation of Product Care®, the industry's product stewardship program; and the founding of the Alliance for Consumer Education, the association's non-profit educational foundation for which he is a member of the Board of Trustees and serves as Secretary. Under Cathcart's leadership the Association has enjoyed a steady growth in membership and has achieved strong financial footing. Cathcart serves in various other capacities within the industry, including as President of the Association's insurance company, Consumer

Specialties Insurance Company (CSI). He is also on the Board of Directors and Secretary of the Consumer Aerosol Products Council and is a board member of the Canadian Consumer Specialty Products Association. Prior to joining CSPA, Cathcart worked for the National Association of Chemical Distributors, beginning in March of 1992 as Vice President and General Manager. He was named Executive Vice President in September of 1993, and President and Chief Operating Officer in December of 1998. From 1990 to 1992, he served as President, Hazardous Materials Advisory Council, and from 1981 to 1990 he served in various management positions with the Chemical Manufacturers Association, now known as the American Chemistry Council. From 1974 to 1981 he served in both military and civilian government positions. He earned his Bachelor's of Science from the United States Military Academy at West Point, a Master's of Arts from Central Michigan University, and completed other postgraduate work at George Washington University. Chris and his family live in Potomac, Maryland. Away from work, Cathcart enjoys sailing, biking and distance running. Additionally, he is a pilot and holds a commercial certificate with multi-engine, instrument, and glider ratings.

William (Bill) G. Higgs,
Co-Founder/Consultant, Mustang Engineering

Bill Higgs is one of three founders of Mustang Engineering, a 5000-person engineering design company serving the energy industry. Upon launching Mustang in 1987, Higgs and his partners envisioned growing to a 50-person company, founding Mustang not only to provide superior and innovative engineering, but also as a way to take care of people and provide them with a sense of belonging. In 1992, Mustang was ranked as the 42nd company in Inc. Magazine's "500 Fastest Growing Companies in America" and was ranked as the number one Engineering firm. Far surpassing their initial goal of 50 people, their vision of taking care of people and being the best reimbursable engineering company has not changed in Mustang's 20+ years. Mustang is currently Houston's largest pure engineering company and a world leader serving the oil and gas industry worldwide.

Besides overseeing Sales and Marketing activities for Mustang, Higgs served as Project Sponsor for the BP Atlantis project, a semi-submersible facility in 6,500 feet of water in the Gulf of Mexico, one of four Deepwater Development projects Mustang performed for BP. He also served as Project Sponsor for Marathon Oil's Alba Phase 2A expansion project which will triple the gas/condensate production at this facility located in Equatorial Guinea. Higgs also served as Project Sponsor for ExxonMobil's Hoover Diana DDCV, a record-setting water depth Gulf of Mexico facility for which Mustang provided topsides facility design.

Other Mustang projects for which Higgs was project manager include Conoco's Ukpokiti FPSO, offshore Nigeria; and BP's MC 109, a fixed platform in 1,000 feet of water in the Gulf of Mexico. In 2001 and 2002, Higgs served on the faculty of Texas A&M's Offshore Summer Research Institute. He was also one of three executives that taught Project Management seminars for senior managers of Petrobras in Brazil.

Higgs, along with Mustang partner Paul Redmon, received the Engineering and Construction Contracting Association's (ECC) 2004 Achievement Award in recognition of "Visionary Leadership in the Process Industry". Higgs has been an invited speaker and panelist at various industry conferences. In February 2006, Higgs was the keynote speaker at Texas A&M's 61st annual Instrumentation Symposium, attended by owner/operator companies in the process and oil and gas industries. At Offshore Europe 2005 in Aberdeen, he gave a presentation titled "Best in Class Project Execution—An Engineer's View". Higgs was a keynote luncheon speaker at OTC 2005, delivering a message entitled "Engineering Drives Projects . . . What Drives Engineering"?

Panels he has served on include project management panels for the Offshore Technology Conference (OTC), the ECC annual conference, and the 2004 annual Rice Global Forum for Engineering and Construction.

Higgs was also the featured speaker in two web casts sponsored by the Southern Gas Association, aimed at engineering in the industry. The first web cast, broadcast in October 2005, was titled "Ethics and Trust Drive Business", and the second web cast, delivered in November, 2006, was "How to Develop Greater Leadership in an Engineering Culture".

Higgs' sense of adventure and practical management and leadership skills started early in life through his involvement in Scouting. He credits scouting for teaching him the ability to create solutions and manage large projects by breaking them down into small tasks, critical skills he would need later in life. Higgs is an Eagle Scout with three palms, and, in March 2005, he was awarded Scouting's prestigious Distinguished Eagle award, an honor bestowed on a very few number of Eagle Scouts throughout the world. Higgs is a 2003 Silver Beaver recipient, and served as Co-Chairman of the Sam Houston Area Council of Boy Scouts' Friends of Scouting (FOS) campaign for four years, 2003-2006. He previously served as Chairman of Division II of Sam Houston Area Council; the nation's largest at 30,000 members.

A 1974 Distinguished Graduate of the United States Military Academy at West Point, he participated in intercollegiate competition in both wrestling and judo and lettered two years as sweeper on the Army soccer team. Higgs graduated in the top 5% of his class at West Point and was runner-up in the Rhodes scholarship competition. Higgs has served West Point as a member of its Board of Directors Fund Committee.

While in the Army, Higgs went to Airborne training, Atomic Demolitions training and is an honor graduate of the Army Ranger School (and King of the Pits!). A Vietnam era veteran, his last job in the Army was Commander of a Combat Engineer company in the First Cavalry Division.

Higgs began his career in the oil and gas industry in 1979 as an engineer, concentrating on offshore Gulf of Mexico projects and working for two local engineering firms before helping launch Mustang in 1987. He received a Texas Professional Mechanical Engineers license in 1987 by testing.

While a considerable share of Higgs' energy is devoted to the privileges and responsibilities of taking care of 5000 Mustangers, he has some energetic ways of vacationing, including mountain climbing in Iceland and Brazil and offroading trips with his son. Higgs also relaxes by doing woodworking, cycling (he has completed several rides in conjunction with the MS-150 program), golfing and playing soccer.

Bill has been happily married to his wife, Ann, for 36 years and has a 32 year old son who is a graduate of Texas A&M University and a 26 year old daughter who is a graduate of The University of Texas in Austin. The Higgs also have a 6 year old granddaughter and 4 year old grandson.

The Higgs reside in Charlotte, North Carolina.

Joshua S. Levine,
Managing Director of Kita Capital Management, LLC

Joshua S. Levine is a Managing Director of Kita Capital Management, LLC, an information technology investing, operating, consulting and research firm, since 2006. He is CTO and a Director of Americans Elect, a non-partisan effort to use the Internet to nominate a presidential ticket for every state ballot in 2012. The website AmericansElect.org won the 2012 SxSW (South by Southwest) People's Choice award, awarded to Groupon in 2011. Started in July 2011, AmericansElect.org had over 3.5 million visitors, 400,000 registered users, 460,000 Facebook fans and 10,000 Twitter followers by March 2012.

From 2007, until its exit with Investment Technology Group (ITG) in 2010, he was the CEO and a Director of ESP Technologies Corp., a financial technology provider to asset managers. He joined ESP as CEO and invested with Credit Suisse, Bear Stearns and Susquehanna Growth Equity. Under his leadership, annual revenues grew from $12 million in 2006 to over $60 million in 2010, and made the Inc. 5000, the Red Herring North America 100, and Deloitte's Technology Fast 500 lists. Levine was also a finalist for the 2009 Ernst & Young Entrepreneur of the Year.

Before ESP, he was the Chief Technology and Operations Officer of E*TRADE FINANCIAL, the online financial services company, where he was responsible for the company's global technology, operations and customer service. In 2001, he moved E*TRADE completely to open-source technologies and a two-second trade execution guarantee.

Levine was a member of the E*TRADE Office of the President and managed the European business, with subsidiaries in the United Kingdom, Germany, Denmark, Norway, Sweden, Israel and South Africa. He brought the European business from a loss of $60 million in 2001 to break-even in 2002 and profitability in 2003. In 2004 and 2005, Europe had the highest growth rate of E*TRADE businesses. He received many industry awards, including InfoWorld's "Top 25 most influential CTO's", CIO magazine's "CIO 100", CIO Forum's "Top 20 financial IT executives", Keynote's best transaction speed and reliability, a "Webby" for the best banking and bill pay on the internet, and an American Business Award "Stevie" for the best technology team.

Before joining E*TRADE in 1999, Levine was Managing Director and Global Head of Equity Technology at Deutsche Bank, where he was responsible for the technology development and systems for the Global Equity division. During his tenure, he successfully integrated two major acquisitions, Bankers Trust and NatWest Markets.

Before Deutsche Bank, he was a Managing Director at Morgan Stanley serving in various leading technology roles for 12 years, both in the business units and in Information Technology, ultimately as CTO.

Levine is currently a board member of Xceedium, a network security appliance company. Previously, he has been a director of Logical Information Machines, a financial technology data provider purchased by Morningstar; Archivas, a storage software company purchased by Hitachi Data Systems; Securify, a network appliance company purchased by McAfee; and StorageApps, a storage appliance company purchased by Hewlett-Packard.

His philanthropic work includes serving as a Director at DonorsChoose.org, connecting philanthropy and public education through technology; a Director of NPower, helping non-profits with affordable IT services; a Director of HappyDoll.org, connecting children in need; and a Young Associate Director of The Metropolitan Opera.

Levine was a member of the National Academies "Committee on Improving Processes and Policies for the Acquisition and Test of Information Technologies in the Department of Defense". He is a former advisory board member to the National Counterterrorism Center in the Dept. of National Intelligence and former Georgia Technology Authority member, appointed by Georgia's Governor for a 3-year term in July 2000.

He co-authored a textbook, "Application Systems in APL", published by Prentice-Hall. Levine is a graduate of the Bronx High School of Science and dropped out of Syracuse University to pursue a career in computing. In 2001, he received an honorary D.Sc. from the University of Georgia, Southern Polytechnic State University. Levine currently holds FINRA license Series 7, 63 and 24.

Patrick A. McBrayer,
President/CEO, AxioMed Spine Corporation

Mr. Patrick A. McBrayer serves as the President and Chief Executive Officer of AxioMed Spine Corporation. Mr. McBrayer served as the Chief Executive Officer of

Xylos Corporation since joining in 2000. Prior to Xylos, he served as President and Chief Executive Officer of Exogen, Inc., which was acquired by Smith & Nephew, Inc. in 1999. Prior to Exogen, Mr. McBrayer served in various executive positions from 1987 to February 1994 at Osteotech, Inc., including President and Chief Executive Officer. Mr. McBrayer guided the Osteotech's transition from its inception to a public entity.

From 1979 to 1986, he served in a variety of positions of increasing responsibility with Johnson & Johnson, Inc., including Marketing Manager of the Patient Care Division, where he built a significant business in surgical products. Mr. McBrayer has over 20 years healthcare senior management experience and served as an Infantry Officer Company Commander in the U.S. Army prior to beginning his business career. Mr. McBrayer is a Founder of Transave Inc. and served as its Chairman of the Board. He served as Chairman of the Board of Xylos Corporation since 2003. He serves as Member of Business Advisory Board at Transave Inc. He serves as a Director of AxioMed Spine Corporation. He served as Director of Transave Inc. He served as a Director of Exogen Inc. since February 1994. He serves as Director of Xylos Corporation. He served on West Point's Association of Graduates Board of Trustees. Mr. McBrayer is a 1974 graduate of the United States Military Academy.

James (Jay) McConville, EVP, Chandler/May, Inc.; Chairman of the Board of AME Unmanned Air Systems, Inc. a Chandler/May company

James (Jay) McConville is the Executive Vice President for Strategy and Business Development at Chandler/May, Inc. and the Chairman of the Board of AME Unmanned Air Systems, Inc. a Chandler/May company. The combined companies specialize in the design, development and manufacture of unmanned aircraft systems (UAS), UAS Ground Control Systems, and Intelligence, Surveillance and Reconnaissance (ISR) mission management solutions for defense and intelligence customers. Mr. McConville is the former President and CEO of AME Unmanned Systems (then called "AeroMech Engineering"), and served four years as the Vice President for Strategy and Business Development for Chandler/May. Before joining Chandler/May, Mr. McConville was the Vice President of Reconnaissance and Surveillance within a major defense firm, directing over $300M per year of the company's systems integration and engineering business. He has served in various other industry positions supporting defense agencies and the national intelligence community for over 15 years.

Prior to entering industry, Mr. McConville served as a United States Army Intelligence Officer, leading both tactical reconnaissance units and analytical organizations, including service with the 1st Cavalry Division during Desert Shield and Desert Storm.

Mr. McConville is the President of the Washington DC Chapter of the Association of Unmanned Vehicle Systems International (AUVSI) and also serves on the Mt. Vernon-Lee Chamber of Commerce Board of Directors.

Mr. McConville has a Bachelors of Science from George Mason University and a Master of Science in Strategic Intelligence from the Defense Intelligence College, Washington, DC.

Ronald J. Steptoe,
Chairman and CEO, The Steptoe Group

Ronald has over 25 years of management, operational, marketing experience in the healthcare advocacy, marketing / public relations industries. He has extensive experience in bringing new medical therapies to market and managing their growth in a diverse array of Government and Private Healthcare Systems. He has received professional credentialing as a Certified Medical Representative (CMR).

Ronald created and managed industry leading multicultural and emerging markets business models for Pfizer's Multi-Cultural Business Team. His area of focus and market specific expertise is in multicultural healthcare. He directed the multicultural marketing and advocacy initiatives for Pfizer's 13,000 sales managers and representatives in the United States.

Mr. Steptoe's has served as the principle negotiating partner for over $ 2 billion in resort development projects in the Caribbean and South East Asia for Federal Owens Development, LLC.

Ronald is the Managing Member and Majority Owner of the Steptoe Group, LLC. He started the Steptoe Group to bring healthcare advocacy curriculum and training to the federal sector marketplace. He is a Service Disabled Veteran and is leveraging his extensive private sector business experience in providing management and technical solutions to the Government and Private sectors with his firm the Steptoe Group, LLC.

As CEO, Ronald has established innovative partnerships with National Medical Association, Department of Continuing Education, Accreditation Council of Continuing Medical Education, and the International Association of Continuing Education and Training to provide a "medically-accredited military culture, cultural competency, and patient-provider communication in the clinical setting" educational training program for health and service support providers with the expertise and capacity to deliver high-quality services that are patient-centered, evidence based and address the health needs of vulnerable population within the military and veteran communities. The Steptoe Group's proprietary business model (Training, Information Management, Communications, and Research / Assessments) addresses the lack of medically-accredited health care provider and practitioner training, educational resources, uniformity and systemic impediments that exacerbate cultural, economic, familial, and regional geographic challenges contributing to disparities in health, healthcare, and services provided to the military and veteran communities.

Ronald serves on the Board of Directors of USA Cares, Inc (a Veterans Service Organization). Prior to joining Pfizer 21 years ago, Ronald served as an officer in the United States Army. He is also a 1987 graduate from the United States Military Academy, West Point, NY.

Lee A. Van Arsdale,
Soldier and Business Executive

Lee A. Van Arsdale has served as a Soldier and business executive. As a Soldier his assignments were primarily in Special Forces, with 11 years spent in the First Special Forces Operational Detachment-Delta (Airborne). In the course of his 25 year Army career, Lee served in three combat zones in leadership positions, and was decorated for valor with the Silver Star and with the Purple Heart for wounds received in combat. Additionally, he participated in numerous classified operations, on a global scale, while in a leadership capacity.

Following his military career, Lee was the Assistant General Manager for National Security Response at the Bechtel Nevada Corporation; he incorporated Unconventional Solutions, Inc., a private consulting firm; he was the founding Executive Director of the University of Nevada Las Vegas Institute for Security Studies, and was the Chief Executive Officer of Triple Canopy, Inc., an integrated security solutions company. He now serves on the boards of select companies.

Don Zacherl,
CEO, T3 Technologies

Don Zacherl founded T3 Technologies in March 2004 based on a number of governing principles that continue to drive its development: Trusted, Talented, and Tireless. Don has extensive leadership and management experience in Military, Non-profit, and Corporate organizations. Don was chosen by "ComputerWorld" magazine as one of the 100 Premier Technology Leaders in the United States.

His company was recognized twice by Dun and Bradstreet 'Open Ratings' for Outstanding Customer Service, 2004 and 2007 and chosen as "Outstanding American by Choice" by the Department of Homeland Security, 2008.

He is a graduate of the United States Military Academy at West Point, earning a Bachelors of Science degree in engineering. He holds an MA in Mathematics and Computer Science from Hofstra University and an MBA from George Washington University. He was selected for Beta Gamma Sigma Honor Society. His other accomplishments include graduating from the CIO Executive Program at Stanford University and completing the Business Model Development program at Aresty Institute of the Wharton School of Business. He is a Microsoft Certified Systems Engineer.; a PMI Certified Project Management Professional (PMP); and a Lean Six Sigma Master Black Belt from Villanova University.

Don's C-suite experience includes: two years as CTO for a Non-Profit Lobbying Organization; three years as COO of a Commercial Software company; and five years as the CEO of a Management Consulting.